Science
Quest
6

Published by
C J Fallon
Ground Floor – Block B
Liffey Valley Office Campus
Dublin 22

First printing May 2006

Acknowledgements
In the case of some photographs, the publishers have been unable to contact the
copyright-holders but will be glad to make the usual arrangements with them, should
they contact the publishers.

Printed in Ireland by
Colour Books Limited
105 Baldoyle Industrial Estate
Baldoyle
Dublin 13

Introduction

For the teacher

This is the **Sixth Class** book in the *Science Quest* series of science activity books.

The *Science Quest* series reflects the changes in content, structure and teaching approaches contained in the science component of the **SESE** Primary School Curriculum.

The *Science Quest* series introduces children to basic scientific concepts, using experiments that are easy to carry out in the classroom and pitched to the children's level. All experiments have been tried and tested in the classroom and each chapter contains Helpful Hints for teachers to pre-empt any difficulties that may arise. Very little expenditure is required by the teachers or pupils for experiment equipment because everyday objects are employed throughout.

This series complements the *Geography Quest* series and the *History Quest* series to provide a comprehensive programme of **SESE** activities to children.

Skills development

◎ The core skills recommended in the Revised Curriculum for Science are widely developed throughout the book.

◎ The skill of **observation** is developed through carrying out the experiments and is tested in the activities that directly follow each experiment (usually **Activity A** and / or **B**).

◎ The skills of **predicting** and **hypothesizing** are promoted in the **Getting Started** and **Prediction** sections of each chapter.

◎ The skills of **investigation** and **experimenting** are developed through conducting the experiments and also in the FIND OUT MORE sections at the end of most chapters.

◎ The skill of **questioning** is promoted in the **Challenge** section.

◎ The skills of **estimating** and **measuring** are developed in certain experiments (e.g. in *Testing for Starch*, *The Tornado Machine* and *Solar Stills*).

◎ The skills of **recording** and **communicating** are developed throughout the book in the EXPERIMENT RECORD sheet which appears in each chapter.

Using this book

This sequence of activities should be followed in each chapter.

The pupil

- ◎ completes the written instructions for the experiment.

- ◎ predicts what he / she thinks may happen in the experiment.

- ◎ carries out the experiment under the teacher's supervision.

- ◎ answers the questions in the activities that follow the experiment.

- ◎ records what happened on the EXPERIMENT RECORD sheet.

- ◎ carries out the **Challenge(s)**, if required, at the end of each chapter.

In the *Science Quest* series

In most cases, the chapters do not have to be followed sequentially. The children are asked to complete the instructions for each experiment — an important innovative feature as it requires them to think scientifically. Questions are logically laid out, progressing from direct observation to analysis and understanding of the concept involved.

FACT BOXES put concepts into a practical and real world context and serve to challenge the children to think more about the concept. The thrust of the book is towards enjoying Science and a beginning of understanding rather than detailed, tedious and confusing explanations of abstract ideas. The aim of this book is to help children to develop a practical appreciation and love of Science.

In this book, children are directed to search the **Internet** for information on various topics. It is strongly recommended that such activities are carried out under teacher supervision. Furthermore, the authors advise teachers to ensure the school's **Internet** settings are set to maximum security.

Contents

Introduction

Chapter Title	Strand Unit	Page
1. Potato Power!	Human life / Plant and animal life	1
2. Hoist away! Simple pulleys	Forces	5
3. Pitfalls and Pooters	Plant and animal life / Environmental awareness	9
4. Slick Tricks	Forces / Properties and characteristics of materials	16
5. Testing for Starch	Human life / Plant and animal life	20
6. Getting your Bearings	Forces / Materials and change	25
7. The Kaleidoscope	Light	29
8. Tornado Machine	Forces	33
9. Aerosol Spray Gun	Forces	37
10. The Electromagnet	Magnetism and electricity / Properties and characteristics of materials / Materials and change	41
11. Circuits and Switches	Magnetism and electricity	45
12. Finding a Balance	Forces	48
13. Chemistry in the Kitchen	Properties and characteristics of materials / Materials and change	52
14. Algae and Fungi	Plant and animal life	58
15. Plant Detectives	Plant and animal life	64
16. Solar Stills	Environmental awareness / Caring for the environment / Science and the environment	68
17. Challenging Times	Light / Heat / Properties and characteristics of materials / Environmental awareness / Science and the environment	75
18. Quiz Time		79

For the pupil

Here are some tips for filling in your
EXPERIMENT RECORD sheet.

- Always draw a clear diagram.

- **Remember** a picture is worth 1000 (or more) words.

- Don't forget to label your drawing.

Make a list of all the things you used in your experiment.
(Hint Look back at your checklist.)

When you write about your experiment say

A. What you did. (Hint Look back at your instructions.)

B. What you thought would happen.

C. What did happen — even if the experiment didn't work!

D. Why you think it happened (or why you think it didn't happen).

E. What you learned. (Hint Look back at your answers to the questions.)

If you can do these, you are thinking like a scientist. **Well done!**

Chapter 1

Potato Power!

Introduction

Our bodies are made up mostly of water.
This water is contained in millions of tiny **cells** in our bodies. Like us, plants are made up of **cells** which are full of water. The cells in plants and animals can dry up, so they must be able to take in more water if they are to survive. The experiment in this lesson shows how living cells dry up. Potatoes are used in this experiment because, like all vegetables, potato cells hold a lot of water.

A. Materials needed

potato

Warning
Be careful when using a knife.

Experiment Time!

B. Look at the pictures and write what you need to do.

Use the words in the brackets to help you.

1. _____

   (into, a potato, Cut, two halves.)

2. _____

   _____

   (in the centre, Scoop out, of each half. a hollow,)

3. _____

   _____

   (centre, some salt, Pour, into the, of one half.)

4. _____

   _____

   (both halves, for about two hours. Leave, in eggcups,)

Strand: Living things.
Strand Units: Human life / Plants and animals.
Objectives: To introduce the children in a simple way to osmosis in plants and humans and to relate it to their own experiences.

1

C. Prediction

What do you think will happen to the potato (a) with the salt in it or (b) with nothing in it?

(a) _____

(b) _____

Now do the experiment.

D. Experiment results

1. Using your hands, touch both potatoes. Which is softer (a) the potato with the salt or (b) the potato without the salt? _____

2. Was the salt wet or dry? _____

3. If the salt was wet, did the water come from (a) the tap, (b) the salt or (c) the potato?

   _____

4. Did the same amount of water come out of the potato without salt? _____

> **The salt drew the water out of the cells of the potato.**

E.

1. If we eat something salty, do we feel (a) cold, (b) thirsty or (c) hungry? _____

2. Does salt draw the water out of the **cells** in our bodies? _____

3. Why do we not drink seawater? _____

   _____

4. What would happen to our bodies if we stopped drinking liquids?

   _____

5. Why do people put moisturising cream on their bodies after sunbathing?

   _____

FUN BOX 1

When we boil potatoes, we kill their cells. Try the same experiment using a boiled potato and see if water can pass from the dead cells into the salt.

FACT BOX 1

Plant and animal cells are made up of over 90% **water**. The remaining 10% is made up of **proteins**, **fats** and **sugar**.

 **EXPERIMENT RECORD**

Draw your experiment. Using the wordbox, label your drawing.

WORDBOX
raw potato
salt
knife
spoon
eggcup

Make a list of what you used in your experiment.

Describe how you carried out your experiment.

Conclusions

FUN BOX 2

Old Wrinkly!

* Carve a face in a peeled apple.
* Put the apple in a bowl of very salty water for a day.
  (This draws the water out of the apple.)
* Take out the apple and leave it in a warm place for about three weeks.
  (Any water left in the apple will evaporate.)
* Decorate **Old Wrinkly** with hair and beady eyes.
  (You can even varnish it if you want it to last!)

FUN BOX 3

Leave two raw potatoes outside for a few days — one peeled, one not peeled. After a few days, compare the potatoes. Which one has lost the most water? Did the skin of the potato help to stop the potato **dehydrating**? Our skin does the same job!

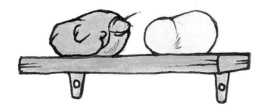

FACT BOX 2
Our skin is like a protective barrier stopping us from drying out entirely!
However, our skin allows some moisture to pass out from our bodies
to cool us down when we are hot. We must replace this lost moisture
by drinking. Indeed, most headaches are caused by **dehydration**
(loss of water). Sipping water throughout the day and especially after
exercise is very important and will stop us dehydrating.

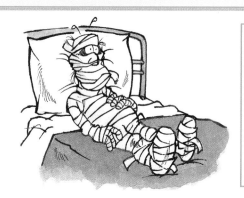

FACT BOX 3
Our skin not only keeps water in, but also prevents
harmful liquids and gases from seeping into our cells
from outside our bodies. When we get a deep cut or
a bad burn, we lose some of this protection. We have
to use bandages or antiseptic creams to protect us
against infection.

FACT BOX 4
As we get older, the cells in our skin become drier
and wrinkles appear! Many people use
moisturising cream to **rehydrate** their skin in an
attempt to retain their youthful complexions!

FACT BOX 5
The ancient Egyptians used a type of salt called
natron to dry out dead bodies as part of the grisly
business of making mummies.

Challenge

Find out how much water there is in an apple?
This challenge requires patience.

 FIND OUT MORE
Use an **encyclopaedia** or the **Internet** to find out more about **osmosis** (the movement of
water in and out of cells).

Integration: Health Education: Caring for our skin, eating and drinking healthily. The importance of fresh foods.
Visual Arts: Making 'shrivelled' heads using apples.

Chapter 2

Hoist away! Simple pulleys

Introduction

Pulling heavy weights uphill can be back-breaking work! It's much easier to pull something downwards using your own weight to help you. Wouldn't it be great if there was a way of lifting something **upwards** without having to do all that hard work? Wouldn't it be even better if, by pulling downwards on something, we could get it to go further upwards? Well, **pulleys** allow us to do just that. In this experiment, we will make a pulley which allows us to move an object upwards by actually pulling downwards.

A. Materials needed

> **Helpful Hint**
> After you tie the string around the book, make sure that there is about two metres of string left to hoist the book around the nail.

Experiment Time!

B. Look at the pictures and write what you need to do.
Use the words in the brackets to help you.

1. _____

(Using a hammer, of the blackboard. into, puts a nail, Teacher, the frame,)

2. _____

(about 2 metres, a piece of string, long, Tie, around a book.)

3. _____

(on the floor, Place the book, pull the string, and, over the nail.)

Strand: Energy and forces.
Strand Unit: Forces.
Objective: To encourage the children to explore how a basic pulley system works and to then use the results of their investigations to redesign and refine their own pulley system.

4. _____

_____

(string. on the, gently downwards, Pull,)

C. Prediction

Can you predict what will happen when you pull downwards on the string?

_____

Now do the experiment.

D. Experiment results

1. What happened to the book when you pulled down on the string?

   _____

2. Was all the string moving in the same direction when you pulled down on it? _____
   Explain. _____

3. Where did the string change the direction in which it was moving? _____

   _____

E.

1. Which do you think takes less effort (a) to lift the book using the pulley or
   (b) to stand on a chair and lift it up by the string directly? _____

   _____

2. Why? _____

   _____

   Try it and see.

3. Which was easier – to lift it up or to use the pulley?

   _____

4. Do you think pulleys change the weight of objects?

   _____

5. What do pulleys change? _____

6. Where in the pulley system is the **turning point** for the change in direction?

   _____

EXPERIMENT RECORD

Draw your experiment. Using the wordbox, label your drawing.

Make a list of what you used in your experiment.

_____

Describe how you carried out your experiment.

_____

_____

Conclusions

_____

_____

Pulleys
are very
old inventions.

What is happening in the picture? _____

Write about how pulleys are being used in this picture, based on life in a Norman castle.

_____

_____

Is there more than one pulley used here? Explain._____

_____

7

Explain how a pulley is used to hoist a flag.

_____

_____

_____

_____

FACT BOX
A special pulley called a **block and tackle** was designed to increase the lifting power when a sailor pulled down on the rope. In the past, block and tackle pulleys were used on sailing ships to help sailors to lift heavy cargoes on board and to help them hoist heavy sails and rigging.

Explain how you think a pulley is used in this picture of a modern elevator (lift).

_____

_____

Challenge

- Can you improve on the basic pulley design by using an old cotton spool or a toy car wheel with its tyre removed?

- Could you design a pulley system that uses more than one turning point? How do you think this will affect the direction in which the string will move?

 FIND OUT MORE
Use an **Internet** search or your classroom **encyclopaedia** to find out more about pulleys, block and tackle and elevators.

Integration: **History**: Building technology of the Normans, sailing ships

Chapter 3

Pitfalls and Pooters

Introduction

Three-quarters of the animals living in the world are minibeasts (often called creepy-crawlies). Many we know very well, such as snails, spiders, butterflies and centipedes. Others are so tiny, we don't even notice them. Unlike mammals, birds and fish, minibeasts have no backbone — they are invertebrates. They are also very adaptable and can be found in every environment, from deserts to mountain peaks to lakes and forests. They have also been around for a long, long time – more than 350 million years in fact! By comparison, humans have been on Earth for about 2 million years! So, set your pitfalls and make your pooters and learn a little more about the incredible world of creepy-crawlies!

Experiment 1 The Pitfall

Helpful Hint
The holes may be dug in an open place in the school grounds.

A. Materials needed

fruit   meat

Experiment Time! **Setting the trap**

B. Look at the pictures and write what you need to do.
Use the words in the brackets to help you.

1. _____

_____

(15cm deep. Dig, in the school, about, two holes, garden,)

2. _____

_____

(jam jars, of the ground. Place, in the holes, with the surface, with the rims level,)

3. _____

_____

(Put, in one jar. a slice of orange, / in the, of meat, Put, a small piece, other jar.)

Strand: Living Things.
Strand Units: Plant and animal life / Environmental awareness.
Skills: Observation, classification, ordering, questioning, recording.
Objective: To teach the importance of close observation and classification when studying and identifying insects.

4. _____

(Place, around both holes. on the ground,
  four stones, / the stones. Put, on top of, a piece of wood,)

5. _____

(a fifth stone, of the wood, Place, on top, it in place. to keep,)

6. _____

(the next day. in the holes, until, Leave, the jars,)

Helpful Hint

The pieces of wood over the pitfalls will protect the minibeasts from rain and direct sunlight. The use of different 'baits' is to attract a wider variety of minibeast.

C. **Prediction**

What sort of minibeasts do you think you might catch during the night in
 (a) the **herbivore** (vegetarian) trap and (b) the **carnivore** (meat) trap?

(a) _____

(b) _____

Now do the experiment.

The next day take in your **pitfall** traps.
Put the lids on the jars and see what you have caught.

Experiment 2 The Pooter

Pooters are clever devices for catching tiny insects without hurting them. You can buy them in School Supply or Science Supply shops, but it is more fun to make your own.

Helpful Hint
Afraid of sucking up a tiny minibeast? Tape a tiny square of muslin around the end of the straw (part in the jar) that you are sucking through for protection.

A. Materials needed

plasticine

Experiment Time! Making a Pooter

B. Look at the pictures and write what you need to do.
Use the words in the brackets to help you.

1. _____

_____

_____

_____

(two straws, plastic bottle. Place, in a, / of the bottle. should be, half in and half out, One straw, / and two thirds out, of the bottle. should be, one third in, The second straw,)

2. _____

_____

(steady, plasticine. in the bottle, with some, Keep the straws,)

3. _____

_____

_____

(in your mouth. the short straw, Hold, / the long straw, minibeast. at the, Point, / on the straw. gently, Suck,)

Find some tiny **minibeasts** to suck into your **pooter**.

Very Important Keep your minibeasts in plastic tubs. Put in some leaves and grass. Cover the tubs with cling film. Don't keep your minibeasts for very long — a few hours at most! Be sure to return them to their natural habitat.

C. **Experiment results**

What have you found? To identify a minibeast, you will have to observe it closely and record your findings. Choose a minibeast to study and answer the following questions.

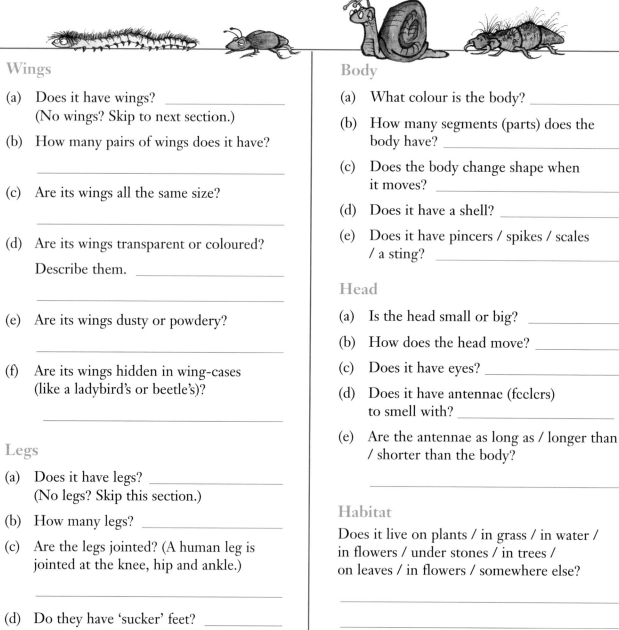

Wings

(a) Does it have wings? _____
(No wings? Skip to next section.)

(b) How many pairs of wings does it have?

_____

(c) Are its wings all the same size?

_____

(d) Are its wings transparent or coloured?
Describe them. _____

_____

(e) Are its wings dusty or powdery?

_____

(f) Are its wings hidden in wing-cases
(like a ladybird's or beetle's)?

_____

Legs

(a) Does it have legs? _____
(No legs? Skip this section.)

(b) How many legs? _____

(c) Are the legs jointed? (A human leg is
jointed at the knee, hip and ankle.)

_____

(d) Do they have 'sucker' feet? _____

Body

(a) What colour is the body? _____

(b) How many segments (parts) does the
body have? _____

(c) Does the body change shape when
it moves? _____

(d) Does it have a shell? _____

(e) Does it have pincers / spikes / scales
/ a sting? _____

Head

(a) Is the head small or big? _____

(b) How does the head move? _____

(c) Does it have eyes? _____

(d) Does it have antennae (feelers)
to smell with? _____

(e) Are the antennae as long as / longer than
/ shorter than the body?

_____

Habitat

Does it live on plants / in grass / in water /
in flowers / under stones / in trees /
on leaves / in flowers / somewhere else?

_____

_____

D.

Now try to identify your **minibeast** using the key below.

(Note Your minibeast may not be listed here, in which case you will have to look up a nature book.)

LEGS

No legs	A **foot** but no legs	8 legs	More than 8 legs	6 legs plus wings or wingcases	6 legs plus **no** wings
Earthworm Larvae of fly	Snail (shell) Slug (no shell)	Spider	Centipede Millipede Woodlouse Caterpillar (suckers on back legs)	Go to **Wings** section below	Earwig Grasshopper (back legs longer than front)

WINGS

1 pair of wings	2 pairs of powdery wings	2 pairs of smooth / transparent wings plus long antennae	2 pairs of smooth wings plus short antennae	2 pairs of wings of different sizes	Wing cases covering body
Fly	Butterfly Moth	Aphid (short spikes on its back)* Lacewing Caddis fly	Dragonfly Mayfly Damselfly	Wasp Bee Ant	Ladybird Beetle

*Aphids (for example, greenfly) do not always have wings.

earthworm snail slug spider centipede millipede woodlouse caterpillar

earwig grasshopper fly butterfly moth aphid lacewing caddis fly

dragonfly mayfly damselfly wasp bee ant ladybird beetle

E.

Choose a minibeast you have identified and draw it accurately. Label your picture.

Draw your minibeast.

13

EXPERIMENT RECORD — Pitfalls and Pooters

Draw your experiments.

Pitfalls	Pooters

Make a list of what you used in your experiments.

Pitfalls _____   **Pooters** _____

_____   _____

_____   _____

_____   _____

Describe how you carried out both experiments.

Experiment **1** _____   Experiment **2** _____

_____   _____

_____   _____

Conclusions

_____

_____

FACT BOX 1

Minibeasts use different ways to protect themselves from predators. **Snails** use shells, while **slugs** are covered in slime, which makes it difficult for birds to pick them up. **Caterpillars** and **grasshoppers** use camouflage, while **ants** and **worms** live under the ground. **Earwigs** and **beetles** have pincers to fight off their enemies while **ladybirds** (and **beetles**) have colours that warn birds that they don't taste nice!

FACT BOX 2

There are 150 000 kinds of **butterflies** and **moths** and these come in all shapes and sizes. The largest moth in the world is the **atlas moth**, which is as big as a frying pan!

Atlas moth

FACT BOX 3

An ant's nest contains hundreds of ants and has many different rooms — some rooms are just for rubbish, others are 'nurseries' for the eggs and the **larvae** (grub, caterpillars). Each nest has a **queen** ant — the rest are **worker** ants. The worker ants guard the nest, look after the nurseries, find the food and fight off enemies. They 'talk' to each other by tapping their feelers together.

FACT BOX 4

Minibeasts that eat plants are **herbivores**, while those that eat other creatures are **carnivores**. **Spiders** are carnivores. The silk from which a spider weaves its web is stronger than steel of the same thickness! Spiders are short-sighted — they 'feel' the movements of the insect in their web through the hairs on their legs.

Challenge

Make a wormery

Gardeners love worms — they mix the soil for them and prevent it getting clumpy and solid. In a **wormery**, you can observe worms at work.

- Put alternate layers of sand and soil in a large glass jar or old aquarium.

- Put in a few fat worms.
  Place a few dead leaves and grass clippings on the top.
  Keep the top of the soil damp.

- After a while (quite a while sometimes), the worms will pull down the leaves into their burrows and, as they do so, they will mix up the sand and soil.

 FIND OUT MORE
Use an **encyclopaedia** or the **Internet** and nature books to find out more about **minibeasts**.

Integration: Visual Arts: Drawing minibeasts.

15

Chapter 4

Slick Tricks

Introduction

When two materials rub against each other, they can cause **friction**. This may be good news when we need something to have a good firm grip but can be bad news for the moving parts of machines. Oils are very good at reducing friction between materials, as they **lubricate** them — they make them slippery. In this experiment, we will explore how to reduce friction and grip using a lubricating oil.

A. Materials needed

Helpful Hint
Do this experiment over a newspaper.

Experiment Time!

B. Look at the pictures and write what you need to do.

Use the words in the brackets to help you.

1. _____

_____

(1m long, a piece, around, of sugar. Tie, of string, a 1kg bag,)

2. _____

_____

(gently, lift, Using the string, the bag of sugar, off the ground.)

3. _____

_____

(on the ground, Replace, and rub, on your hands. the bag of sugar, some cooking oil,)

4. _____

_____

(again, try, the bag of sugar. to lift, Now,)

Strand: Materials / Energy and forces / Materials.
Strand Units: Forces / Properties and characteristics of materials.
Objectives: To encourage the children to explore and investigate how friction and traction (grip) can be reduced by lubricants and to encourage them to evaluate how lubrication can be countered by using oil-absorbent materials such as talcum powder.

C. Prediction

Can you predict how well you will be able to lift the bag of sugar when you have oil on your hands?

_____

_____

Now do the experiment.

D. Experiment results

1. What happened when you tried to lift the bag of sugar the first time? _____

_____

2. What happened when you tried to lift the bag of sugar with oil on your hands? _____

_____

3. What difference did the oil make to your grip? _____

_____

E.

1. What does oil do to the surface of materials? _____

_____

2. How would this affect them when they rub or grip each other?_____

_____

3. Why do you think car mechanics often wipe their hands with a cloth before they pick up heavy tools? _____

_____

4. Why do you think an oil spill on a road can be so dangerous? _____

_____

After carrying out this experiment, you may notice that your hands are still quite oily and slippery. Wash them with **soap** and water.

What did the **soap** do to the oil on your hands? _____

_____

Many everyday machines need oil to work properly. Look at these pictures and say why oil is important to these machines.

Car engine

_____

_____

_____

Bicycle chain

17

EXPERIMENT RECORD

Draw your experiment. Using the wordbox, label your drawing.

Make a list of what you used in your experiment.

_____

Describe how you carried out your experiment.

_____

_____

_____

Conclusions

_____

_____

The Professor has decided to lubricate his mountain climbing ropes.
Do you think he is doing the correct thing? Why?

_____

_____

FACT BOX 1

Water can also act as a lubricant. If enough rainwater builds up on a road, it can act as a layer between the road and the tyres of cars trying to grip the surface. If the tyres lose their grip on the road, the cars may skid and slide as though they were on ice. This is called **aquaplaning** and can cause serious accidents. Drivers should always reduce speed in wet conditions to avoid the danger of aquaplaning.

FACT BOX 2

This workman is spreading sand over an oil spill on a road. The sand soaks up the oil and allows tyres to get a good grip on the road surface.

These children have placed a strip of plastic sheeting on a piece of level ground (it works best if the ground is soft and grassy). Having poured a few buckets of water onto the plastic sheeting, they now have a very good water slide.

What effect has the water on the plastic sheeting?

_____

_____

Challenge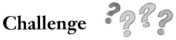

Try to repeat the oil and string experiment, but see if you can counter the lubricating effect of the oil by rubbing flour, talcum powder or chalk dust onto your hands, as well as the oil.

Can you now explain why weightlifters rub powder onto their hands before they attempt a lift?

_____

_____

 FIND OUT MORE
Use an **encyclopaedia** or the **Internet** to find out more about **friction**.

Integration: **SPHE**: Road safety.

Chapter 5

Testing for Starch

Introduction

Plants, unlike animals, can make their own food. Plants use the energy of the Sun to make food, which they usually store in the form of starch. Starch gives energy to the plant. This starch is the 'fuel' that feeds the plant and helps it to grow. Starch also gives energy to us when we eat the fruit, roots or stems of plants. In this experiment, we will use an iodine solution to test foods (and other items) to see if they contain starch.

A. Materials needed

kitchen paper

dropper

saucer

Flour

cardboard

cheese

plastic bag

potato

sugar

Salt

pasta

Helpful Hints

Tincture of iodine and dropper bottles are available from pharmacies. Iodine will need to be diluted prior to the lesson (**1** drop of iodine to **20** drops of water). **Iodine is a poison and should not be tasted —** dispose of the items tested after the lesson. To avoid staining clothes and work surfaces, use a newspaper and old clothes. Close adult supervision is recommended during this experiment — some teachers may prefer to do this as a demonstration lesson.

B. Look at the pictures and write what you need to do.

Use the words in the brackets to help you.

1. _____

   (on a table. 12 saucers, Put,)

2. _____

   (a small sample, on a, Place, of each item, separate saucer.)

diluted iodine

3. _____

   (into a dropper. Put, iodine, some,)

Strand: Living things / Materials.
Strand Units: Human life / Plant and animal life.
Objective: To conduct a test for starch and show its origin in plants.
Skills: Predicting / testing / experimenting / observing / recording / classifying / analysing.

4. _____

_____

(of iodine, a drop, Put, sample. on each,)

- If the drop of **iodine** turns blue / **black** when it touches the item being tested, there is **starch** present.

- If the drop of iodine remains its normal colour (brown), there is no starch present.

C. Prediction

Write the colour you predict the iodine will turn in the chart below.

ITEM	Prediction Will iodine turn — (a) blue / **black** or (b) remain brown?	What happened? Did iodine turn — (a) blue / **black** or (b) remain brown?
apple		
cheese		
pasta		
tissue		
cardboard		
paper		
sugar		
salt		
flour		
biscuit		
bread		
plastic		

Now do the experiment.

D. Experiment results

1. Complete the chart above.

2. What colour is iodine? _____

3. What colour does iodine change to when mixed with starch? _____

4. List the items you tested that contained starch: _____

_____

5. List the items you tested that did not contain starch: _____

    _____

6. How many predictions did you get right? _____

E.

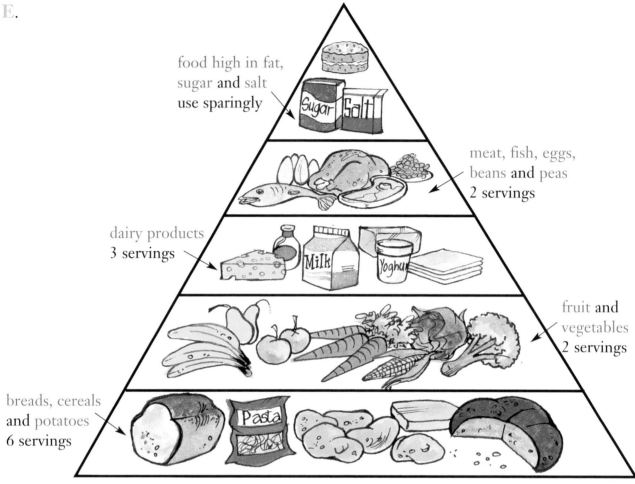

food high in fat,
sugar **and** salt
use sparingly

meat, fish, eggs,
beans **and** peas
2 servings

dairy products
3 servings

fruit **and**
vegetables
2 servings

breads, cereals
and potatoes
6 servings

1. Look at the food pyramid. Are starches found in many foods? _____
    (Test more foods if you need to.)

2. To which part of the food pyramid do foods containing starch belong? _____

3. Carbohydrates are a very important part of our diet. The **starch** in carbohydrates
    releases energy slowly into our bodies throughout the day and keeps us active.
    Write suggestions for a good carbohydrate-rich breakfast for a hard-working student.

    _____

    _____

    _____

potatoes   wheat

rice

FACT BOX 1
Foods which contain a lot of **starch** are
often the **staple** (the main food) of
people in poor countries.

FACT BOX 2
Different parts of the world have different staple foods. Use this map of the World to help you to find out which food is the most important in each part of the World.

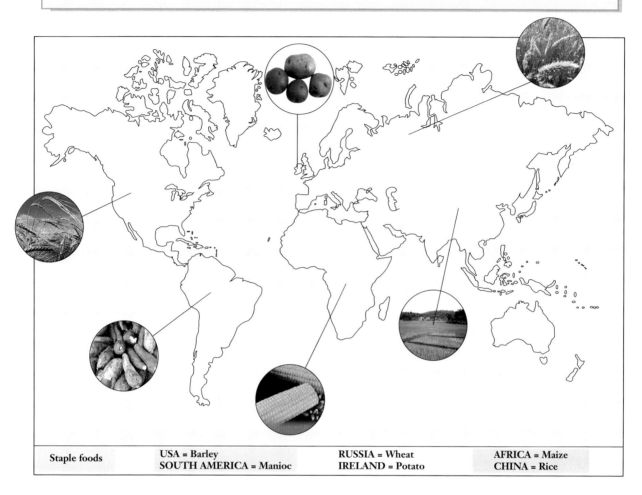

| Staple foods | USA = Barley | RUSSIA = Wheat | AFRICA = Maize |
| | SOUTH AMERICA = Manioc | IRELAND = Potato | CHINA = Rice |

FACT BOX 3
If people depend too much on one staple food and that crop fails, famine is often the result. This happened in Ireland in the 1840s when potato blight destroyed the potato crop, which was the staple food of the Irish people.

FACT BOX 4
Starch is more than just a food. It is also used to stiffen clothes. It comes as a white powder and when it is added to a clothes wash, the clothes become very smart and stiff! In the past, it was used to give gentlemen's shirts a very stiff crease.

EXPERIMENT RECORD

Draw your experiment. Using the wordbox, label your drawing.

WORDBOX
iodine
jar
12 saucers

Make a list of what you used in your experiment.

_____

_____

Describe how you carried out your experiment.

_____

_____

Conclusions

_____

_____

Challenge

Starch is an important part of our diet but a diet of starchy foods alone would be unbalanced. Your challenge is to design a healthy, balanced lunch for your lunchbox.

FIND OUT MORE
Use the **Internet** or an **encyclopaedia** to research **famines in history**.
Try to find out what caused them.

Integration: **SPHE**: Looking after your body by eating healthy foods.
History: Studying famines and their causes — over-reliance on staple foods.
Geography: Identifying staple foods across the World.

Chapter 6

Get your Bearings

Introduction

When moving objects rub against each other, they can cause **friction**. Over time, this friction may result in wear and tear on the moving objects. Machinery often fails to work or breaks down because of this friction. One way of reducing friction between objects or the moving parts in machines is to use **bearings**. Bearings act like a slippery 'filling' when sandwiched between two surfaces that would otherwise rub against each other. In this experiment, we will discover how bearings work.

A. Materials needed

marbles

B. Look at the pictures and write what you need to do.
Use the words in the brackets to help you.

1. _____

_____

(some books, on the floor. in a pile, Place, / of books. Using, the pile, one finger, try to move,)

2. _____

_____

(on the floor, Place, each about 2cm apart. pencils, about ten,)

3. _____

_____

(on the pencils. Place, of books, the pile,/ with one finger. Now, the pile, try to push, of books,)

Strand: Energy and forces / Materials.
Strand Units: Forces / Materials and change.
Objectives: To encourage the children to explore how bearings reduce friction and to apply what they have learned through their investigations to build a device that uses bearings to operate properly.

25

4. _____

_____

(on the floor. about 30 to 40 marbles, Arrange, / on the marbles. the pile, of books, Place,)

5. _____

_____

(using one finger, pile of books, push the, on the marbles. Now,)

C. Prediction

What do you think will happen when you try to move the books on a bare floor? _____

_____

What will happen when you try to move the books on the pencils? _____

_____

What will happen when you try to move the books on the marbles? _____

_____

Now do the experiment.

D. Experiment results

1.   When I tried to push the books along the bare floor, it was _____.
     (easy, hard, impossible)

2.   What happened when you tried to push the books, using the pencils? _____

_____

3.   What happened when you tried to push the books, using the marbles? _____

_____

E.

1.   Was it easier to move the books on the marbles or on the pencils? Explain why.

_____

_____

2.   Which set-up would be the best to use if you wanted the books to move in only
     one direction? _____

3.   Which set-up would be the best to use if you wanted the books to move in many
     different directions? _____

EXPERIMENT RECORD

Draw your experiment. Using the wordbox, label your drawing.

WORDBOX
marbles
pencils
books
finger

Make a list of what you used in your experiment.

_____

Describe how you carried out your experiment.

_____

_____

Conclusions

_____

_____

(a) What is likely to happen to the Professor? _____

(b) Do you think it is easy to predict which way she might fall?_____

(c) Why? _____

27

FACT BOX 1
The ancient Egyptians used large wooden rollers, which they made from trees, to move huge stones, weighing many tonnes, when they built the Pyramids. The rollers worked in much the same way as the pencils did in your experiment.

Challenge

Build a bearing racing cart

You can have fun with a tea tray and marbles if you turn the tray upside down over the marbles. Make sure that the rim of the tray isn't deeper than the size of the marbles.

(a)   Why? _____

(b)   What should happen when you give the tray a little push? _____

_____

You could build a number of tray racing carts and attach a mascot to each one. A number of pupils could push these at the same time to race them.

What kind of surface would be the best on which to race your carts?

_____

_____

FIND OUT MORE
Investigate how **ball bearings** are important in **rollerblades**, **skateboards** and **bicycles**.

Integration: **History**: Ancient Egypt — Building the Pyramids.
Geography: Modern Egypt.

Chapter 7

Kaleidoscope

Introduction

When you look in a mirror, you see a reverse image of yourself. Everything is reversed… but what would you see if one mirror reflected the image of another mirror? Photographers and TV companies sometimes create **special effects** using mirrors. Magicians perform many of their **illusions** and tricks with mirrors. In this experiment, you will be able to work a little magic of your own.

A. Materials needed

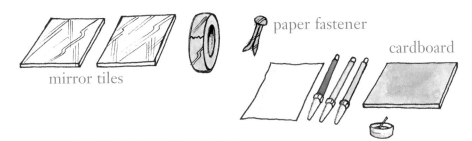

mirror tiles

paper fastener

cardboard

Helpful Hint

If you are getting mirror glass cut for this experiment, make sure that the edges are smoothened to avoid cuts. The best mirrors for this experiment are mirror wall tiles. They can be purchased cheaply in most DIY stores and have already-smoothened edges.

B. Look at the pictures and write what you need to do.

Use the words in the brackets to help you.

1. _____

_____

(a right angle. two mirrors, Join, some sticky tape, with, in the shape of,)

2. _____

_____

(coloured markers. Decorate, using, a piece of paper,)

3. _____

_____

(of the decorated paper. through, Put, a paper fastener, the centre,)

Strand: Energy and forces.
Strand Unit: Light.
Objectives: To encourage the children to observe how light reflects and how this reflection affects the images we see, also that the children may apply what they have learned to design and build a simple periscope device.

4. _____

_____

(to the, with a paper fastener. the decorated page, Join, cardboard base,)

5. _____

_____

(the paper fastener. Place, of the mirrors. on top of, the right angle,)

6. _____

_____

(the mirrors. and, Rotate, the decorated paper, look at,)

C. **Prediction**

Can you predict what will happen when you rotate the paper? _____

_____

Now do the experiment.

D. **Experiment results**

1. How many mirror images could you see? _____

2. Were all the images the same? _____

3. How did they differ? _____

4. How did the images change as you rotated the paper? _____

5. Did the images have symmetry? _____

E.

1. Do you think the images would change in any way if you were to change the angle made where your two mirrors meet? _____ Try it and see.

2. Have you ever seen optical effects like this in a film or on TV?_____
   Where? _____

3. Light a candle and place it close to your mirror kaleidoscope. How many candle flames do you see? _____

4. Do you think the mirrors increase the light given out by the candle? _____

_____

5. What do you think you would see if you were to make a kaleidoscope, using three or even four mirrors? _____ Try it and see.

 # EXPERIMENT RECORD

Draw your experiment. Using the wordbox, label your drawing.

WORDBOX
two mirrors
tape
paper
pencils
markers
cardboard

Make a list of what you used in your experiment.

_____

Describe how you carried out your experiment.

_____

_____

Conclusions

_____

_____

FACT BOX 1
Flashlights and headlights on cars use reflective curved mirrors behind the bulbs to increase the light given out.

The real da Vinci Code

The great artist and scientist, **Leonardo da Vinci**, kept many of his discoveries secret by writing his notes in a very clever way. He wrote in **code** but also reversed the letters and words. They could only be read by holding the writing up to a mirror. Then the reversed writing could be seen in the correct way.

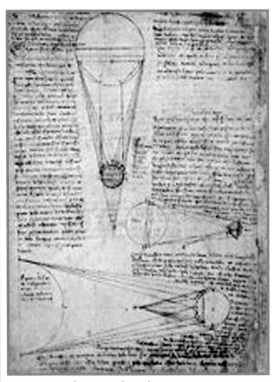

The codex hammer

You might like to get a spare photograph of yourself and set it up in your kaleidoscope. Everyone will then see you in a completely new way!

See yourself as you really are.
Explain how you can use two mirrors to see yourself as you really appear and not as a mirror image.

FACT BOX 2
The **periscope** is a tube that works using **two** mirrors. Periscopes use two mirrors, one at the top of a tube and another at the bottom, to give a true image to the viewer. Periscopes allow people in submarines to see what is happening on the surface of the sea while the submarine is submerged in water. In the Second World War, German U-boats sank hundreds of ships by using periscopes to help them to locate their targets on the surface.

FACT BOX 3
One of the oldest working **periscopes** in the world is the one used in the famous **Camera Obscura** in Edinburgh. Visitors can sit in a darkened room while the periscope projects live images of the city onto a screen. No video cameras are used.
It is all done using daylight and mirrors.

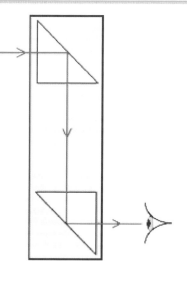

Challenge

- Can you design and build your own simple periscope?

- Suggested materials include… two small mirrors, cardboard and sticky tape.

- It is best not to make one that is too long — about 30cm would be fine. The trick is to make sure that the mirrors face each other properly.

- Look at the diagram. It will give you ideas on how to set up your mirrors.

FIND OUT MORE
Use an encyclopaedia or log onto **www.scoilnet.ie** to find out more about periscopes and kaleidoscopes.

Chapter 8

Tornado Machine

Introduction

When a liquid is poured out of a bottle, two things happen. Firstly, the liquid comes out of the bottle. Secondly, air goes up into the bottle to replace the liquid that is coming out. This is why you often hear a 'glug, glug, glug' as a bottle empties in a sequence of 'liquid out, air in, liquid out, air in' until the bottle is empty.

There is a quicker way of emptying a bottle if you use the correct force. In this experiment, we are going to build a sealed unit that will show how to pour a liquid quickly but will also show what a tornado looks like. We are going to build a tornado simulator.

A. Materials needed

colouring

Helpful Hint
The stronger you make the joining of the two bottles the better.

B. Look at the pictures and write what you need to do.

Use the words in the brackets to help you.

1. _____

_____

(a, Half fill, with water. plastic bottle,)

2. _____

_____

(some, Put, into, food colouring, the bottle with the water.)

3. _____

_____

(with the water. Place, on top of, an empty bottle, the bottle, / tops of the bottles, the, meet, Make sure, perfectly.)

Strand: Energy and Force.
Strand Units: Forces / Centrifugal force.
Objectives: That the children should build a device to help them to observe how a vortex behaves and to relate their observations to the world around them.

4. _____

_____

(the tops, Join, strong tape. of the bottles, with,)

5. _____

_____

(upside down. the water flow. the bottles, Turn, and let,)

6. _____

_____

(them, the bottles, again, spin, Now, upside down, turn, but this time, in a circular motion.)

C. Prediction

What will happen when you (a) hold the bottles still and let the liquid simply fall and (b) spin the bottles to stir the liquid as it falls?

_____

Now do the experiment.

D. Experiment results

1. Describe how the water poured into the bottom bottle when you held the bottles still. _____

_____

_____

2. Describe how the water poured when you swirled the bottles around quickly.

_____

_____

_____

3. Which method worked the better – the first or the second? _____

4. In what way did the water look like a tornado? _____

_____

E. 1. What did you notice rising up through the water in the top bottle the first time?

    _____

    2. Did you notice any air bubbles the second time you tried the experiment?

    _____

    3. When I swirled the bottles, the water travelled down in a _____.
        (straight line, spiral)

    4. As the water spiralled downwards, it _____.
        (went down the side of the bottle, got stuck, evaporated)

    5. Because the water travelled down the sides of the bottle _____
        was able to go easily up into the top bottle to take its place. (more water, air, my thumb)

FACT BOX 1
Tornadoes look just like the swirling water you made in your simulator, except that tornadoes are made of air that is spinning at hundreds of **kilometres** per hour. However, just like your water model, a tornado is a hollow tube of spinning material. Air rises up through it with incredible speed and force.

A tornado

EXPERIMENT RECORD

Draw your experiment. Using the wordbox, label your drawing.

| WORDBOX |
| two bottles |
| water |
| tape |
| food colouring |

Make a list of what you used in your experiment.

_____

Describe how you carried out your experiment.

_____

_____

Conclusions

_____

_____

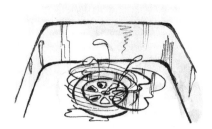

FACT BOX 2
When water pours down the plughole in a sink, it acts in a similar way to a tornado. The Earth's rotation is what causes the water to swirl around. In the **Northern Hemisphere**, water pours **clockwise** down a plug hole. In the **Southern Hemisphere**, the water flows **anticlockwise**.

Can you guess which way water goes down a sink **exactly** on the Equator?

_____

_____

FACT BOX 3
Another word for a spinning column of gas or liquid is a **vortex**. A tornado is a type of **vortex**. You created a vortex in the tornado simulator you built.

FACT BOX 4
Strong currents in the sea or in fast flowing water sometimes cause **whirlpools**. Objects and people tend to get sucked down under water if they are caught in a whirlpool.

FACT BOX 5
In a galaxy, the gravity of hundreds of millions of stars can also cause them to move in a giant spiral.

A spiral galaxy

Challenge

Your challenge is to see whether water flows down more quickly if the tornado simulator is spun faster.

- How will you test this question?
- How will you time your test?
- What do you think the result will be?
- Do the actual results match your prediction?

FIND OUT MORE
Use your classroom **encyclopaedia** or the Internet to find out more about **tornadoes** and **whirlpools**.

Integration: **Geography**: Extreme weather conditions — tornadoes.

Chapter 9

Aerosol Spray Gun

Introduction

Fast-moving currents or jets of air can have strange effects on still, calm air around them. In some cases, fast jets of air will cause still, calm air to move in very strange ways. In this experiment, we will use currents of fast-moving air to create an aerosol spray gun.

A. Materials needed.

Helpful Hints

You might like to use some sticky tape to keep the two pieces of straw in the shape of a right angle. It is important that when you blow into the long piece of straw, the air moves straight across the top of the shorter piece of straw.

B. Look at the pictures and write what you need to do.

Use the words in the brackets to help you.

1. _____

_____

(with, a small plastic bottle, Fill, water.)

2. _____

_____

(a plastic, Cut, straw, from the top. about a third distance / the straw. Do not cut, fully through,)

3. _____

_____

(so as to make, Bend, a right angle. the straw,)

Strand: Energy and Forces.
Strand Unit: Forces.
Objective: To encourage the children to explore and investigate the effect of fast-moving streams of air on still air and to apply what they have learned to create a paint spray device.

4. _____

_____

(the short end, the bottle of water. of the straw, into, Put,)

5. _____

_____

(straw. Blow hard, of the, the long end, through,)

C. **Prediction**

What do you think will happen when you blow hard through the long end of the straw?

_____

Now do the experiment.

D. **Experiment results**

1. The air in the long piece of straw _____ across the top of the short piece of straw. (jumped, blew, tripped)

2. Some water from the bottle was _____. (lost, sprayed, spilled)

3. The harder I blew, the _____ water was sprayed. (more, less)

4. About how far did the water spray? _____

E.

1. Do you think the water was pushed up or sucked up by the fast jet of air you blew?

_____

2. What happened to the water as soon as it was drawn into the jet of air?

_____

3. If a fast jet of air blows across a pipe or a tube, it can _____.
(suck air out of it, make it bend, break it)

FACT BOX 1
Professional spray guns
work in much the same way
as the device you have made.

The Professor wants to paint this wall but has forgotten his brush.

Please give him some helpful suggestions. _____

_____

EXPERIMENT RECORD

Draw your experiment. Using the wordbox, label your drawing.

Make a list of what you used in your experiment.

_____

Describe how you carried out your experiment.

_____

_____

Conclusions

_____

_____

FACT BOX 2

Chimneys work in a similar way to the spray gun.
Wind blows across the top of the chimney and
draws up air. This is how smoke is drawn away
from a fire and out into the air outside.

FACT BOX 3

This old perfume bottle was used to spray perfume.
Ladies used to squeeze the little rubber ball when
they wanted to spray perfume on to their faces.

Can you explain how this might have worked?_____

_____

FACT BOX 4

When skyscrapers were first built, people
noticed they worked like powerful chimneys
whenever the doors at ground level were
opened. Powerful gusts of wind would gush
into the buildings, sometimes causing great
damage. Airtight, revolving doors were
invented to prevent these currents of air
blowing through the building.

Can you explain how these revolving doors worked?_____

_____

Challenge

Make your own aerosol gun to spray paint in Art Class.
The paint will have to be watery or it will be too difficult to blow.

You might like to combine a spraying of weak watery paint over pastel or chalk drawings
where you can create some interesting dappled effects. It's a good idea not to overdo the
spraying when attempting this.

FIND OUT MORE
You might like to research the work of artists who use **spray guns** rather than **brushes**
in their work. Airbrushing is a highly skilled art form and **airbrush art** can achieve
very realistic results.

Integration: **History**: Inventions from the past.
40   **Visual Arts**: Spray painting and the work of airbrush artists.

Chapter 10

The Electromagnet

Introduction

Magnets are made from iron or from materials that have iron in them.
You will find magnets in nature — for instance, the Earth's core (rock at the centre of the Earth) is a giant magnet. This is a type of magnetic iron rock called magnetite. Scientists have even found tiny amounts of this magnetite in the brains of birds, such as pigeons. It seems these birds have their very own built-in compasses in their heads!

We can make magnets by stroking a piece of iron very carefully with a magnet. Another way of making a magnet is to use electricity. In this experiment, we will learn how to use electricity to make a magnet.

A. Materials needed

Helpful Hint

Make sure that the battery terminals are connected to **bare** wire ends. Otherwise the current will not flow through the wire and the electromagnet will not work.

B. Look at the pictures and write what you need to do.

Use the words in the brackets to help you.

1. _____

_____

(close to, a long nail, paperclips, Hold, some, and thumb tacks. pins,)

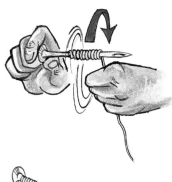

2. _____

_____

(in, the nail, one hand. Hold, / some copper wire, the nail, wrap, around, Using your other hand, about 50 times.)

3. _____

_____

(about 10cm, at either end, Leave, of wire, of the nail.)

Strand: Energy and Forces.
Strand Units: Magnetism and electricity / Properties and characteristics of materials / Materials and change.
Objective: To encourage the children to explore how an electric current can be used to generate a magnetic field and how this may be used to create an electromagnet.

4. _____

_____

(of the copper wire, Connect, the ends, of the battery.
to both terminals,)

5. _____

_____

(hold, the pins, paper clips, and, the nail, Now, close to,
thumbtacks.)

C. **Prediction**

What do you think will happen? _____

_____

Now do the experiment.

D. **Experiment results**

1. Did any of the metal objects stick to the nail the first time you tried it? _____

2. What was running through the wire when you connected it to the battery?

    _____

3. What happened to the nail when you did this? _____

    _____

4. Did any metal objects stick to the nail the second time you tried it? _____

    _____

E.

1. What did the electric current do to the nail? _____

2. Was the electric current travelling through the nail or through the wire? _____

3. What can happen to iron objects if they are close to an electric current? _____

    _____

4. If only **some** of the metal objects stuck to the nail, what could you say about the
    objects that didn't stick to the nail? _____

    _____

5. Will the nail remain magnetic after you have disconnected the wire from the battery?

    Try it and see.

EXPERIMENT RECORD

Draw your experiment. Using the wordbox, label your drawing.

WORDBOX
copper wire
long nail
small battery
paper clips
pins
thumbtacks

Make a list of what you used in your experiment.

_____

Describe how you carried out your experiment.

_____

_____

Conclusions

_____

_____

FACT BOX 1

A magnet that is made using electricity is called an **electromagnet**.
This crane is using an electromagnet to lift heavy metal objects.

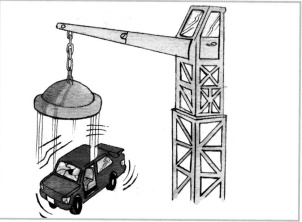

How do you think the crane operator is controlling the lifting and dropping operation?

_____

FACT BOX 2
Many security doors use a
type of electromagnet to
open a lock in a door.
You simply press a button
on a desk and the
electromagnet pulls back
the lock and the door
automatically opens.

Challenge

- A magnetic screwdriver can be a very useful tool. You can use it to hold a screw in position without having to use your other hand. It will also pick up small metal objects from awkward places where your fingers cannot fit. Let's make one.

- You will need a screwdriver with a steel shaft and a fairly strong magnet.

- Stroke the screwdriver along its length about twenty times, using the magnet. The best way to magnetise the screwdriver is to start at exactly the same point each time and to stroke the screwdriver slowly and steadily with the magnet.

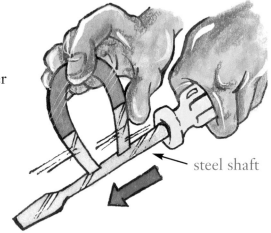

steel shaft

1. See if you can make another magnetic tool using a magnet.

2. List other objects or tools you could magnetise in this way.

FIND OUT MORE
Log onto **www.scoilnet.ie** and find out about **magnets** and **electromagnets**.
You might also like to find out more about how **birds** find their way on **long journeys**.

Integration: **History**: The history of the crane / Great sailors and explorers of the past / The history of the motor car.

44

Chapter 11

Circuits and Switches

Introduction

We use technology to put scientific ideas into practice. Technology uses the discoveries made by scientists to make useful and practical machines and gadgets. It is often said that technology is the appliance of science.

Challenge

In this chapter, you and your group are the **technologists**, using your scientific knowledge of simple **electrical circuits** and **switches** to make working models.

Your **challenge** is to build one (or more) of the following:

1. a lighthouse	2. a steady-hand game	3. traffic lights
4. a quiz game	5. disco lights	

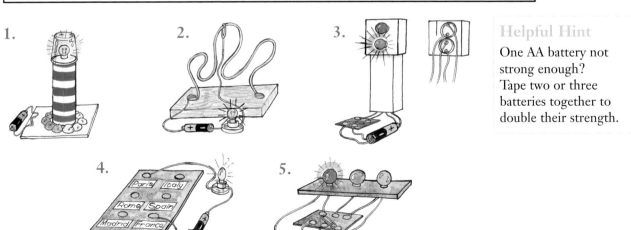

Helpful Hint

One AA battery not strong enough? Tape two or three batteries together to double their strength.

Strand: Energy and Forces.
Strand Unit: Magnetism and electricity.
Skills: Designing, making, ordering, questioning, co-operating, organising, analysing, experimenting, measurement.

Getting started

1. Where possible, it is best to work in groups of 4 to 6.

2. Agree on the **project** you would most like to do.

3. Complete the **Design** and **Materials needed** sections.
   (The diagrams are only meant as a guide.)

4. Decide on your **Building plan**.
   This means deciding what you need to do first (**step 1**), second and so on…

5. When you have your materials gathered, begin your project!

6. When you have finished your project, draw and label a picture of your work.
   (You might like to include a photograph instead.)

7. Finally, make suggestions as to how you could improve your model
   if you were to make it again.

(If you need to refresh your memory on electrical circuits and switches, look back at
Science Quest 5, Chapters **Switch On**, **Switch Off** and **The Great Conductor**.)

OUR CHOSEN PROJECT _____

Materials needed

Building plan

Step 1 _____

_____

Step 2 _____

_____

Step 3 _____

_____

Step 4 _____

_____

Step 5 _____

_____

EXPERIMENT RECORD

Draw your experiment. Using the wordbox, label your drawing.

Make a list of what you used in your experiment

_____

Describe how you carried out your experiment.

_____

_____

Conclusions

_____

_____

The changes I would make if I made the model again.

_____

_____

_____

_____

_____

_____

_____

_____

_____

_____

Draw a picture of your completed model.

Integration: Visual Arts: Designing and making models / **Mathematics:** Ordering and measurement.
SPHE: Co-operation / Working in teams / Developing social skills.

47

Chapter 12

Finding a Balance

Introduction

The Earth's gravity pulls everything and everybody down to the ground.
Weight measures the pull of gravity. The more an object weighs, the stronger the pull of gravity on it. All objects, people and animals have a centre of gravity — this is the part where their weight is centred. The centre of gravity is the balancing point of an object, person or animal. If you push a book very slowly off a table and stop pushing the book just before it is about to fall, you have stopped it at its balancing point or centre of gravity.

A.

In the following experiments, you will see what happens when your centre of gravity is **off-centre**!

Experiment Falling Over!

Experiment Time!

B. Look at the pictures.

Stand sideways beside a wall. Make sure that the side of your shoe and your arm and shoulder are touching the wall. Now try and lift your leg (the leg not touching the wall), without moving your shoe or shoulder from the wall.

Stand with your back against the wall. Make sure your heels are firmly against the wall. Now try to touch your toes, without moving away from the wall.

Stand back to back with your friend. Make sure your heels are touching. At exactly the same time, you both try to touch your toes, without moving your feet!

Strand: Energy and Forces.
Strand Unit: Forces.
Objectives: To develop an understanding of gravity and show the relationship between the centre of gravity and balance.
Skills: Observation / Making / Predicting / Questioning / Experimenting / Recording.

Now do the experiment.

C. Experiment results

1. Could you (a) lift your leg when standing sideways to the wall?_____
   (b) bend forward with your back to the wall? _____

2. What happened when you and your friend tried to touch your toes while back to back?

   _____

3. Could you perform the actions if you could move your body? _____

4. What prevented you from moving your body while doing the experiments? _____

   _____

You won't fall over, if your weight is evenly balanced on both sides of your centre of gravity — just like these identical twins on a see-saw!

Is the centre of gravity of the see-saw at A, B or C? _____

5. Place an X at the centre of gravity (the balancing point) on these pictures.

EXPERIMENT RECORD

Draw your experiment. Using the wordbox, label your drawing.

WORDBOX
two pictures
book
car

Make a list of what you used in your experiment.

_____

Describe how you carried out your experiment.

_____

_____

Conclusions

_____

_____

FACT BOX 1
You would expect that a double-decker bus should topple over when it leans going around a sharp bend. However, because it is built with most of its weight close to the bottom (the wheels and the heavy chassis) and is light on top, it has a **low** centre of gravity. Consequently, a double-decker bus is stable.

FACT BOX 2
Isaac Newton discovered gravity in 1666 when he saw an apple fall from a tree. Science is sometimes about asking obvious questions that nobody has bothered to ask before! So be patient the next time a young child asks you 'why? why? why?'

FUN BOX 1

Balancing clowns, which don't topple over, work in the same way as a double-decker bus — they have a **low** centre of gravity. You can make your own clown quite easily. All you need is a ping-pong ball, plasticine and the cardboard tube from a paper towel.

1. Cut the ping-pong ball in half.

2. Put plasticine in one of the halves, making sure it doesn't fall out.

3. Tape the half with the plasticine to the bottom of the cardboard tube.

4. Tape the other half to the top of the cardboard tube.

5. Draw the clown and gently push him over!

FUN BOX 2

Jumping Jelly Beans have a **moving** centre of gravity. A small ball bearing rolls up and down inside them. When you get tired of your toppling clown, you can turn him into a Jumping Jelly Bean!

1. Remove the plasticine from the ping-pong ball and roll it into balls small enough to roll easily, up and down the cardboard tube. (You could use marbles instead.)

2. Tape the other half of the ping-pong ball onto the top of the tube.

3. Standing the tube on one end, allow it to tumble down a gentle slope. It should flip from top to bottom as the centre of gravity moves up and down the tube.

Challenge

Can you balance a cork on the end of a pencil (without sticking the point into the cork)?

Solution Stick two forks into the sides of the cork — this will make it easier to find the balancing point.

FIND OUT MORE
Find out more about **balancing tricks** by looking up **Magic Trick** books and the **Internet**.

Integration: **Visual Arts:** Making balancing toys. **P.E.:** Exploring movement and balance.

Chapter 13

Chemistry in the Kitchen

Introduction

Many of the everyday **mixtures** in our homes are **chemicals**. Some of these 'chemicals' are **acids**, others are **bases** and some are **neutral** (neither acid nor bases). When acids and bases mix, they cancel each other out. For example, if you mix a few drops of vinegar (acid) with some bread soda (base), they fizz. The result is neither an acid nor a base. It is a neutral. To test whether a solution is an acid, base or neutral, a scientist uses **litmus paper**. We call litmus paper an **indicator** because it indicates to us whether a chemical is acidic, basic or neutral. In this experiment, you can make your very own **indicator** from red cabbage!

A. Materials needed

sieve

Helpful Hints

There is no need to get all the above materials. Red cabbage is often sold in quarters. This is sufficient. Be careful using the knife. The hot water is tap water and should not be too hot.

Experiment Time!

B. Look at the pictures and write what you need to do.

Use the words in the brackets to help you.

1. _____

_____

(cuts, into small pieces. Teacher, red cabbage, some,)

2. _____

_____

(the top, cuts off, Teacher, empty plastic milk container. of an,)

Strand: Materials.
Strand Units: Properties and characteristics of materials / Materials and change.
Objective: To test for acids and bases in common household solutions.
Skills: Testing, observation, predicting, questioning, analysing, classifying and recording.

3. _____

(the empty, into, plastic milk container. Put, of red cabbage, the pieces,)

4. _____

(from the tap. the container, Fill, with hot water,)

5. _____

(the mixture, with a spoon. Stir, in the container,)

6. _____

(for about, the mixture, 1 hour. Leave, to cool,)

7. _____

(into a jug. the mixture, Drain, through a sieve,)

8. _____

(Put, into 10 separate jars. 10 of the above liquids, / jar. each, Label,)

> **Helpful Hint**
> Put liquid into each jar until it is about half-full.

9. _____

(some cabbage water, Pour, each jar. into,)

C. **Prediction**

Can you predict what colour each household liquid will change into when you add the cabbage water? Write your prediction in the chart on the following page.

Cabbage water plus	Prediction Solution will turn (a) **red/pink**, (b) remain the same colour (**purple**), (c) blue/blue-green/yellow-green.	What happened? Solution turned: (a) **red/pink**, (b) remained the same colour (**purple**), (c) blue/blue-green/yellow-green.
vinegar		
water		
baking soda		
lemonade		
baby shampoo		
lemon juice		
coke		
washing-up liquid		
dishwasher liquid		
washing powder		

Now do the experiment.

D. Experiment results

Fill in what actually happened in the table above.

acid   **neutral**   **base**

Helpful Hint
Vinegar is an acid, water is neutral and baking soda is a base — so test these solutions first to see which colour the cabbage water turns when mixed with **acids**, **neutrals** and **bases**.

E.

1. **Acids** turn cabbage water **red** or **pink** (the stronger the acid, the **redder** it gets).
    Which of the solutions you tested were acidic? _____

2. **Neutrals** do not change the colour of the cabbage water.
    Which of the solutions you tested were neutral? _____

3. **Bases** turn cabbage water blue (or blue-green or yellow-green if they are weak).
    Which of the solutions you tested were bases? _____

    _____

FACT BOX 1

The word **acid** comes from the Latin word **acidus** meaning 'sour' or 'sharp to the taste'. Acids usually taste sour or sharp – think of lemon juice or vinegar. Some acids are so strong that they are extremely dangerous to eat or drink.

FACT BOX 2

Acids can conduct electricity. Batteries that are old and corroded often leak acid and should not be touched, as the acid can burn your skin.

FACT BOX 3

Emissions from factories and cars can pollute the atmosphere and affect the rain, making it slightly acidic. When this **acid rain** falls, it destroys crops instead of helping them to grow.

FACT BOX 4

Nettle stings are acidic, but the juice of dock leaves is basic. So if you get a nettle sting, rub it with a wet dock leaf to ease the sting. The acid in the sting is 'neutralised' by the basic dock leaf. On the other hand, wasp stings are basic and so we use an acid, vinegar, to neutralise the sting. Jellyfish stings are treated with vinegar, so are they acidic or basic?

FACT BOX 5

We have very strong acid in our stomachs which helps us digest food — so strong, in fact, that it could actually strip paint off a car! We get indigestion when we have too much acid in our stomach. One cure for this is to eat a little bread soda, which is a base.

55

Professor Botchitt is trying to clean these dirty coins.
She knows that acid is a good cleaning agent, so which jar
should she put the dirty coins in?
(Check your answer by doing the experiment yourself.)

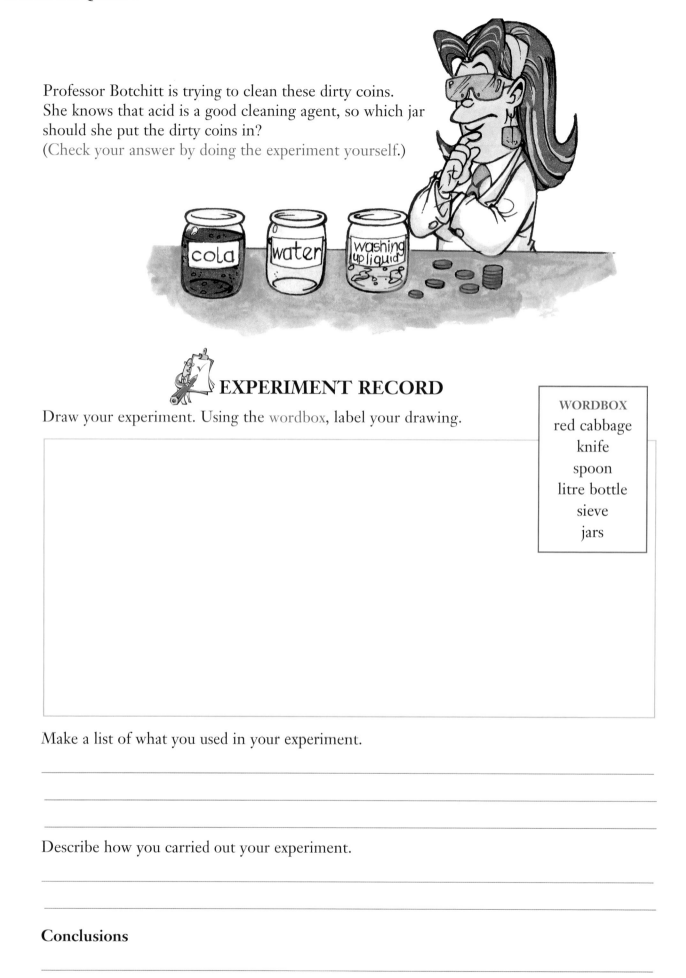

EXPERIMENT RECORD

Draw your experiment. Using the wordbox, label your drawing.

WORDBOX
red cabbage
knife
spoon
litre bottle
sieve
jars

Make a list of what you used in your experiment.

_____

_____

_____

Describe how you carried out your experiment.

_____

_____

Conclusions

_____

_____

Challenge

Your challenge is to see if you can change the colour of red cabbage water.

- When we breathe out, the air contains carbon dioxide.
  Try gently blowing bubbles into a jar of red cabbage water through a straw
  (the colder the water, the better).

- After a few minutes, the cabbage water should start to change colour.
  This is because carbon dioxide dissolves in water and makes **carbonic acid**. The carbon dioxide in your breath dissolves in the water, so the water becomes a very weak acid.

- The change in the colour of the cabbage water shows there is acid in it.

Helpful Hint
The fizz in fizzy drinks is dissolved carbon dioxide.

Helpful Hint
Hold your breath for about 20 seconds before blowing into the straw. The longer you hold your breath, the more carbon dioxide you exhale.

FIND OUT MORE
Use an **encyclopaedia** or the **Internet** to find out more about acids, neutrals and bases.

Integration: Geography: Rainfall throughout the world / Devastation caused by acid rain.
SESE: Proper disposal of dangerous waste.

Chapter 14

Algae and Fungi

Introduction

Fungi grow everywhere! They can even grow on our bodies. Although some types of fungi look like plants, they are very different. Fungi do not need light in order to grow. Also, fungi have no leaves, roots or flowers. They can cause diseases but may also cure diseases. Fungi feed on dead and decaying matter. Welcome to the wonderful world of fungi! Let's start by growing some.

A. Materials needed

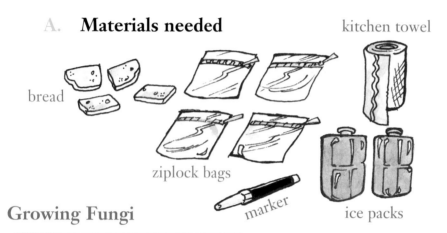

bread

ziplock bags

marker

kitchen towel

ice packs

Helpful Hints

The cool bag is not strictly necessary — a cool corner of the room will do. Two ice packs will allow you to replace the ice pack in the bag every day. The use of four samples allows the orderly elimination of variables and helps to develop scientific method. You may need to re-dampen the paper towels after a day or two. Use slices of bread from the same sliced pan.

Growing Fungi

Experiment Time!

B. Look at the pictures and write what you need to do.

Use the words in the brackets to help you.

1. _____

_____

(the, bags, ziplock, Label, A, B, C and D.)

2. _____

_____

(of kitchen towel, some squares, water. with, Dampen,)

3. _____

_____

(kitchen towel. of, some squares, Fold / the ziplock bags, them, into, marked A and B. Place,)

Strand: Living Things.
Strand Units: Plant and Animal Life.
Skills: Observation, questioning, estimation, prediction, ordering etc.
Objective: To learn about the fungi kingdom.

58

4. _____

_____

(on top of, a slice of, Place, stale bread, kitchen towel, the damp, in ziplock bags, A and B.)

5. _____

_____

(of stale bread, marked C and D. in the, a slice, Place, ziplock bags,)

6. _____

_____

(near a radiator. and leave them, bags A and C, Seal, on a table,)

7. _____

_____

(into bags B and D, and seal them. Put an ice bag, / in a cool place, out of the light. Leave them,)

8. _____

_____

(all the bags, Leave, five days. for about,)

C. Prediction

Which slice of bread do you think will have the most fungi (mould) on it after five days – bread in bag **A** / bag **B** / bag **C** or bag **D**? _____

Now do the experiment.

After five or six days, check your bags and see was your prediction correct.

D. Experiment results

1. Which growing conditions were created in each bag?
Write the letter of the bag beside the correct 'conditions'.

Cool and moist	bag _____	Dry and cool	bag _____
Warm and moist	bag _____	Warm and dry	bag _____

2. Place the slices of bread in order, the one with the most mould first.

Bag _____   Bag _____

Bag _____   Bag _____

> **Helpful Hint**
> The bread in the damp bag near the heat (**bag A**) should have the most fungus, as fungi love warm, wet conditions.

3. Which did you discover were the best conditions for growing fungi? _____

Choose from the options in D **1** _____

> **FACT BOX 1**
> Plants use sunlight, heat and moisture to make their own food. Fungi depend on things such as decaying plants, leaves, stems, trees and logs for their food.

> **FACT BOX 2**
> Plants cannot survive without sunlight. Fungi, on the other hand, prefer damp, dark conditions in order to survive. Mushrooms, which are members of the fungi family, grow at night.

E. 1. Think of a reason why fungi do not need to make their own food.

_____

2. Fungi thrive in dark places and plants do not. Explain why.

_____

3. Mildew and blackspot are names for fungi that grow on plants and flowers. Why do you think gardeners spray their plants and flowers with **fungicides** during hot, damp weather?

_____

_____

4. Fungi digest almost anything. They grow really well in dark, damp places like a forest floor. What do you think would happen to the floor of a forest after a few years if fungi did not do their essential work of digesting rotting and decaying materials?

_____

_____

5. Did you notice a blue fungus on the pieces of bread in your experiment? This is called **penicillium**. It is made into an important antibiotic called **penicillin**. For what are antibiotics used?

_____

> **FACT BOX 3**
> There are at least 100 000 species of fungus. Some even grow on us! Warm, damp runners provide the ideal conditions for the fungal infection *athlete's foot* which mainly affects the skin between the toes.

Mushrooms are perhaps the most well-known form of fungus (fungus is the singular of fungi). They grow in dark, damp places. By studying mushrooms, you will learn how fungi reproduce.

Mushrooms (like all fungi) start life as tiny **spores**.

Millions of these **spores** blow away from the parent mushroom.

When a **spore** lands on moist soil, tiny fibres begin to grow out of it.

When the conditions are right – warm and damp – new mushrooms will grow on the web of fibres.

Professor Messitup is hoping to collect mushrooms to study in his lab. He isn't likely to find any.

Why not? _____

_____

Truffles

Toadstools

EXPERIMENT RECORD Fungi

Draw your experiment. Using the wordbox, label your drawing.

WORDBOX
stale bread
plastic bags
kitchen towel
cool bag
ice packs
marker

Make a list of what you used in your experiment.

Describe how you carried out your experiment.

Conclusions

FUN BOX

Looking at mushroom spores

A mushroom produces up to 40 million spores each hour for about two days. However, these spores are microscopic in size.

If you remove the stalk from a mushroom and leave it gills down on a piece of paper, you should see a pattern of spores.

Challenge

Using the same method as you used for growing fungi in your experiment, try growing fungi on other foods such as carrots, apples, cheese etc.

Record and compare the different fungi that grow on each food item.
Note the colour and types (hairy / fuzzy / slimy etc.) of fungi that grow.

Fruit

Grow fungi on different types of bread (white bread / brown bread / soda bread / homemade bread etc).

Record and compare the differences in the fungi growing on each bread.

Bread

FIND OUT MORE

Find out more about the **fungus kingdom** by looking up the **Internet** or an **encyclopaedia**.

Integration: **SPHE**: Bodily hygiene plus importance of antibiotics.
Visual Arts: Making spore prints.
History: Irish Famine / How hot, moist conditions cause fungal infection / Potato blight.

Chapter 15

Plant Detectives

Rainforest

Introduction

Plants grow in all parts of the Earth. There are millions of different **species** (kinds) of plant. Without plants, no animal could live.
All plants need to make seeds for the next generation, to ensure that the species survives. In this chapter, you will design a series of experiments to find out what conditions seeds need in order to **germinate** and to grow. To make sure the experiment is fair and that it gives the correct result, you need to use exactly the same material and measures.
That way, if you remove one of the materials from the experiment, you can easily tell what effect it has on the result.

Experiment 1 Do seeds need **water** to start to grow?

A. **Materials needed**

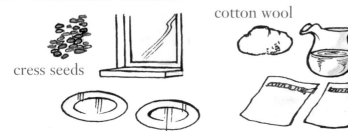

cotton wool

cress seeds

ziplock bags

Helpful Hints

Cress seeds are perfect for this experiment because they germinate within a couple of days. You could seal your experiments in two clear, plastic bags that will maintain the conditions you want to test, without worrying about any water evaporating.

This experiment has two parts to it. In order to achieve a 'fair' result, there can only be one difference between the two parts of the experiment.

What is the one thing you want to test here? _____.
Remember the first part of the experiment includes water while the other part excludes water. Everything else in the two separate tests must be the same.

 Experiment Time!

B. **Draw your experiment.**

part 1 – with	part 2 – without
Record your results.	Record your results.

Strand: Living things.
Strand Units: Plant and animal life. **Skills**: Exploring, planning, making predictions, observing and recording.
Objectives: To encourage the children to think scientifically and to design tests that will assist them to investigate and record the typical conditions for seed germination.

Experiment 2 Do seedlings require **light** to grow healthily once they have germinated?

A. **Materials needed**

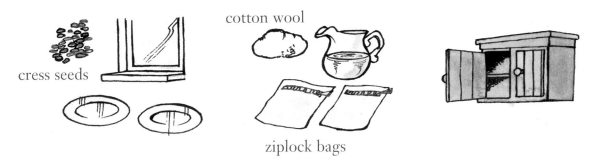

cotton wool

cress seeds

ziplock bags

What is the one thing you want to test here? _____

Remember to design the experiment in two parts, one with **light** and one without light.

Experiment Time!

B. **Draw your experiment.**

part 1 – with	part 2 – without
Record your results.	Record your results.
_____	_____

Remember to give the seedlings time to grow once they have germinated.

Experiment 3 Do seeds need **warmth** to germinate and grow well?

A. **Materials needed**

Helpful Hint

This experiment may have to be carried out at home if the school does not have a warm, dark place and a cold, dark place.

What is the one thing you want to test here? _____

Remember to design the experiment in two parts, one with **warmth** and one without warmth.

Experiment Time!

B.   **Draw your experiment.**

part 1 – with	part 2 – without
Record your results.	Record your results.
_____	_____

Remember to give the seedlings time to grow once they have germinated.

Looking back

1.   What three things about growing seeds did you test?

   Experiment 1 _____

   Experiment 2 _____

   Experiment 3 _____

2.   From what you learned doing these experiments, write a report on what you think are the best conditions in which seeds will grow well.

   _____

   _____

   _____

   _____

   _____

   _____

3.   Do you think the seeds of plants that live in cold countries need exactly the same conditions as the seeds of plants that live in warm countries? _____

   Explain why. _____

   _____

4.   What do you think happens to plants that are suited to growing in dry countries rather than wet countries?

   _____

   _____

Challenge

The cress seeds you used in your experiments germinated quickly. Most seeds take longer. If you were to try to grow the seeds for such plants as nasturtium or calendula, you would find that they would take up to a few weeks to start growing.

You would also discover that not all the seeds start to grow at the same time. Some grow quickly while others are 'programmed' to take longer.

1. Can you think of any reasons why it's a good idea for the seeds of a plant not to germinate at the same time? _____

_____

2. What do you think would happen to the seeds if there was a severe frost?_____

_____

Talk about this in class.

Try to grow nasturtium or calendula seeds for your school garden, if you have one.

The flowers on these plants are edible and look attractive in salads.

Nasturtium

FIND OUT MORE
Run an **Internet** search or log onto www.scoilnet.ie and look for further information on growing seeds. Look up interesting plant records in The Guinness Book of Records. Can you find out what plant makes the world's largest seed?

Integration: Visual Arts: Drawing.
Geography: Plants from different lands / Climate.

Chapter 16

Solar Stills

Introduction

Solar stills use the heat of the Sun to distil – clean and purify – water that is dirty or salty. In Ireland, water is cleaned using water filters but in hot countries, the Sun may be used to distil dirty water.

Solar pool

In the following **two** experiments, you will make two different types of **solar still**. You can then compare the stills and decide which you would prefer to use, if you were in a place where there was no fresh water.

Solar still 1

A. Materials needed

Helpful Hint

When placing the top of the drinks bottle back on the base, make sure that it goes **inside** the sides. Otherwise, the condensation will drop onto the table instead of into the base. The bottle may be left in the sun for a number of days and observed each day to see if there are any changes in the amount of water distilled.

Experiment Time!

B. Look at the pictures and write what you need to do.

Use the words in the brackets to help you.

1. _____

_____

(the base off, drinks bottle, a plastic, Cut, about 12cm tall. leaving it,)

2. _____

_____

(some soil, Mix, into a glass, is half full, which, of water.)

3. _____

_____

(the glass, Place, into, of the, the base, of dirty water, plastic bottle.)

Strand: Environmental awareness and care.
Strand Units: Environmental awareness / Caring for the environment / Science and the environment.
Skills: Comparing / Making / Recording / Predicting / Testing / Analysis / Questioning
Objective: To teach water distillation and purification using a natural resource i.e. the Sun.

68

4. _____

_____

(the top part, plastic bottle, of the, Place, over the base. /
the lid, bottle. on the, Leave,)

5. _____

_____

(in the sun, the bottle, for about, Leave, three hours.)

C. Prediction

What do you think will happen to the water in the glass if you leave it in the sun
for long enough? _____

_____

Now do the experiment.

D. Experiment results

Solar still 1

1. Could the Sun's rays shine through the bottle? _____

2. Did the sides of the bottle get wet / remain dry? _____

3. Did the water in the glass remain at the same level / dry up? _____

4. What happened to the dirt in the water? _____

_____

5. Did water appear in the bottom of the big bottle? _____

6. If water did appear, was it clean and where did it come from? _____

_____

7. Explain in your own words how **solar still 1** works. _____

_____

_____

_____

_____

EXPERIMENT RECORD

Draw your experiment. Using the wordbox, label your drawing.

WORDBOX
small glass
scissors
water
soil
spoon

Make a list of what you used in your experiment.

Describe how you carried out your experiment.

Conclusions

Solar still 2

A. **Materials needed**

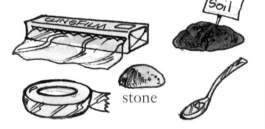

stone

Helpful Hint
To properly compare
the effectiveness of each
'still', you need to put
the same amount of
dirty water in each still
and leave both outside
in the sun at the same
time and for the same
length of time.

Experiment Time!

B. **Look at the pictures and write what you need to do.**
Use the words in the brackets to help you.

1. _____

_____

(water, Put, it is, until, in a mixing bowl, about 3cm deep.)

2. _____
   _____
   (into, the water, Stir, mixing bowl. some soil, in the,)

3. _____
   _____
   (Place, dirty water. in the, an empty glass, /
   should, The water, about halfway, come up, glass. on the,)

4. _____
   _____
   (with cling film. the mixing bowl, Cover,)

5. _____
   _____
   _____
   _____
   (a small rock, Place, directly, over the glass. on the cling film, /
   Place, for about, the mixing bowl, 3 hours. in the sun,)

C. Prediction

What do you think will happen to the dirty water when you leave the bowl in the sun?

_____

Now do the experiment.

Helpful Hints

The rock should form a small hollow to allow the condensation to drip into the glass.
The cling film should not touch the glass.

D. Experiment results

Solar still 2

1. Could the Sun's rays shine through the plastic cling film? _____
2. Did the underside of the cling film become wet / remain dry?_____
3. Did the water in the bowl remain at the same level / dry up?_____
4. What happened to the dirt in the water?_____
5. Did water collect in the glass? _____

6. If water did collect in the glass, was it clean and where did it come from?

    _____

7. Why was it necessary to place a small stone on the cling film over the glass? _____

    _____

8. Explain in your own words how you think **solar still 2** works._____

    _____

    _____

    _____

E.

Solar still 1	Solar still 2

1. Did both solar stills make clean water? _____

2. Which solar still worked the better? _____

3. How do you know? _____

F   1. Use the words in the box to fill in the gaps.

evaporate   **distil**   **impurities**   **condenses**   **vapour**

    A solar still uses sunlight to _____ water. The Sun's rays shine through

    the clear plastic and cause the water to _____. The water _____

    rises, leaving the impurities in the water behind, until it reaches the plastic.

    The water vapour _____ on the plastic and drips back down into

    the glass (or the bottom of the bottle). The water is now clear of _____.

    2. Do you think a solar still could distil clean water from salty water?_____

        _____

        Check your answer by doing the experiment.

    3. Why would knowing how to make a solar still
        have been useful to sailors on long voyages in
        the past?_____

        _____

        _____

4. How could solar stills be useful now in hot, underdeveloped countries?

_____

_____

EXPERIMENT RECORD — Solar stills 1 and 2

Draw your experiments.

Solar still 1	Solar still 2
plastic bottle still	bowl and cling film still

Make a list of what you used in your experiments.

Solar still 1 _____   Solar still 2 _____

_____   _____

_____   _____

_____   _____

Describe how you carried out both experiments.

Experiment 1 _____   Experiment 2 _____

_____   _____

_____   _____

_____   _____

Conclusions

_____

_____

FACT BOX 1

Solar stills have been around for a long time! The first known use of solar stills was by Arabian alchemists back in 1551. Alchemists practised an early form of chemistry where they tried to turn metals into gold. The first modern solar still was designed by a Swedish engineer, **Charles Wilson**, in 1872. He used a solar still in Chile to provide clean drinking water for a mining community.

FACT BOX 2
Solar stills copy the way in which nature makes rain. Solar stills use natural evaporation by the sun and condensation. You could say that the entire world is a giant solar still!

FACT BOX 3
Most of the water on Earth is salt water (97%) and of the remaining 3% fresh water, 2% is in solid form, frozen into glaciers! That leaves just 1% of the Earth's water to be used by humans and animals for drinking or to grow crops.

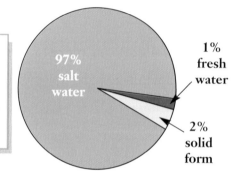

97% salt water

1% fresh water

2% solid form

FACT BOX 4
Humans need about 30-50 litres of fresh water every day for drinking, cooking, cleaning etc. In the developed world, we each use approximately 300 litres of water per person per day. In Africa, every person uses approximately 10 litres of water per day. Every year, about 3·5 million people die from diseases caused by **contaminated** (dirty) water.

Collecting water in Africa

Challenge ???

Survival in the desert!

Your situation is desperate. You have completely run out of water. Can you distil water directly from the ground? Try it and see. Some day it might just save your life.

Integration: **SPHE**: Global differences in water / Wealth distribution.
Geography: The water cycle — salt versus fresh water.

Chapter 17

Challenging Times

Introduction

Science teaches us about the world around us and how it works. We use technology (computers, telephones, machines, cars etc.) to help us to make our scientific knowledge work. In the coming years, we will have to face the problem of finding sufficient energy to keep our technology going. The fossil fuels (turf, gas, oil etc.) which we have used for many years will have to be replaced by renewable (wind, sun, sea etc.) energy sources in order to maintain our technology. In the challenge following, you will explore how the sun, wind and running water may provide the answer to our future energy problems.

Challenge

To build one or more of the following:

1. a wind-powered car

2. a water turbine

3. a solar cutting beam

4. a solar-powered heater

5. a wind turbine

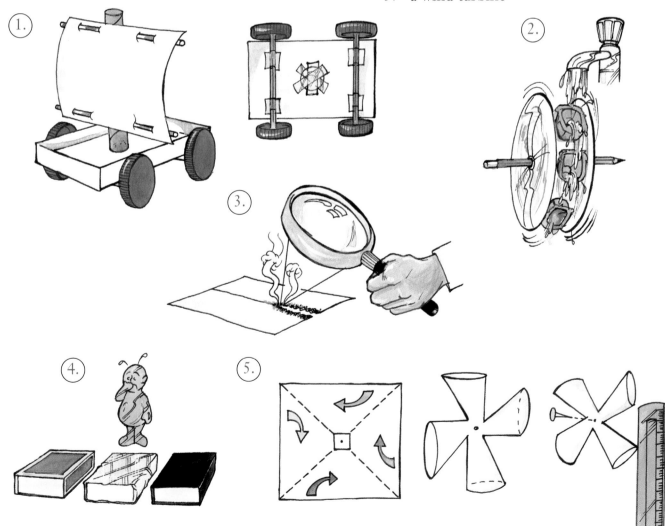

Strand: Energy and forces / Materials / Environmental Awareness and care.
Strand Units: Light / Heat / Properties and characteristics of materials / Environmental awareness.
Objectives: To encourage the children to think scientifically; to develop problem-solving skills and their faculty for design and construction.

Getting started

1. Where possible, it is best to work in groups of from 4 to 6.

2. Agree on which **project** you would most like to do.

3. Complete the **Design** and **Materials needed** sections.
   (The diagrams are only meant as a guide.)

4. Decide on your **Building plan**.
   This means decide what you need to do first (**step 1**), second and so on…

5. When you have your materials gathered, begin your project!

6. When you have completed your project, draw and label a picture of your work.
   (You might like to include a photograph instead.)

7. Finally, make suggestions as to how you could improve on your model,
   if you were to make it again.

OUR CHOSEN PROJECT _____

Materials needed

_____

_____

_____

_____

_____

_____

_____

Design of project

Building plan

Step **1** _____

_____

Step **2** _____

_____

Step **3** _____

_____

Step **4** _____

_____

Step **5** _____

_____

 **EXPERIMENT RECORD**

Place your labels in the wordbox.

Draw your experiment.

WORDBOX
_____
_____
_____
_____
_____

Make a list of what you used in your experiment.

_____

Describe how you carried out your experiment.

_____

_____

Conclusions

_____

_____

The wind car

1. Should heavy or lightweight materials be used to build the car?_____

2. Would large or small wheels work better?

_____

3. Where will you test the car?

_____

4. What is the best way of 'catching' the power of the wind? _____

Yachts

Water turbine

The water turbine

1. Cardboard will work but would other waterproof materials be better?

_____

2. What should you use as a source of running water to test your turbine? _____

77

The solar-powered heater

1. Will a dark object absorb (take in) more of the Sun's heat than a shiny material? _____

2. What should you cover two small boxes with to test this theory? _____

3. What will you put into the heater as a test?

   _____

   (Hint Jelly Babies are great for this!)

4. Where will you test your heater?

   _____

Solar-powered car

Solar cutting beam

The solar cutting beam

1. Can you focus the rays of the Sun into a tight beam of light that will burn through a piece of paper?

   _____

2. Could you move the beam of light to cut a pattern you have marked on the piece of paper?

   _____

3. Why is it important to wear sunglasses when you work with the light beam?_____

   _____

The wind turbine

1. Will light paper work better than heavier cardboard?

   _____

2. How large should you make the turbine?

   _____

3. How will you attach the turbine fan to its support so that it will move freely when the wind blows it?

   _____

   _____

Wind turbine

Conclusions

1. Did your model 'work'?

   _____

2. What changes would you make if you made the model again?

   _____

3. What 'helpful hints' would you give to someone who wanted to make this model?

   _____

Integration: Visual arts — construction.
Objective: Geography: Solar wind, water energy.

Skills: Planning, designing, making, exploring and evaluating.

78

Time to show off!

How good a scientist are you? Now is the time to show off all that you have learned doing the experiments in this book. You can check your answers by looking back at the chapter listed after each question. Write the answers to the questions in your science copybook.

1. Which of these foods contain starch: potatoes / salt / apples / pasta?   (Chapter 5)

2. What can happen to iron when it is put close to an electric current?   (Chapter 10)

3. If a fast jet of air blows across a pipe or tube it can
    (a) suck air out of it, (b) make it bend or (c) break it?   (Chapter 9)

4. Which would work the best to push books across a bare floor in one direction only
    (using marbles / using pencils / using your finger)?   (Chapter 6)

5. What do you think are the best conditions in which to grow seeds?   (Chapter 15)

6. Mark the centre of gravity with an ✕ on this picture   (Chapter 12)

7. Do images seen in a kaleidoscope have symmetry?   (Chapter 7)

8. How many legs have spiders?   (Chapter 3)

9. What does a solar still use to distil water?   (Chapter 16)

10. Can the Sun separate salt from water? Explain.   (Chapter 16)

11. What colour do acids turn red cabbage water?   (Chapter 13)

12. When you use a pulley, is the string always going in the same direction?   (Chapter 2)

13. When you swirled the bottles of your 'tornado simulator', did the
    water travel into the lower bottle in (a) a straight line or (b) a spiral?   (Chapter 8)

14. What will salt do to the water in the cells of our bodies?   (Chapter 1)

15. What will oil do to the surface of materials?   (Chapter 4)

16. Which of these is an acid and which is a base (lemon juice, baking soda)?   (Chapter 13)

17. How do we test foods for starch?   (Chapter 5)

18. What minibeast has a 'foot' but no legs?   (Chapter 3)

19. In what ways could **solar stills** be useful in hot countries
    that do not have a clean water supply?   (Chapter 16)

20. Why do fungi not have to make their own food?   (Chapter 14)

SCORE ____ **/20**

THE GREAT FACT BOX QUIZ

See how many questions you can answer. When you have completed the quiz, check your answers by looking back at the FACT BOXES in each chapter.

1. What do acidic solutions taste like? _____(Chemistry in the Kitchen)

2. Why do double-decker buses not topple over when going around sharp bends?
   _____(Finding a Balance)

3. Why were 'block and tackles' used on sailing ships in the past?_____
   _____(Hoist Away: Simple Pulleys)

4. What happens when a car aquaplanes? _____(Slick Tricks)

5. What is the famous **Camera Obscura** and where would you find it?
   _____(Kaleidoscope)

6. In which direction does water go down a bath plughole in the Southern Hemisphere?
   _____(The Tornado Machine)

7. What is the largest moth in the world called? _____(Pitfalls and Pooters)

8. What does starch do to clothes? _____(Testing for Starch)

9. Approximately what percentage of our bodies is made up of water? _____(Potato Power)

10. What do you call a magnet that uses electricity? _____(The Electromagnet)

11. Why do skyscrapers have revolving doors? _____(The Aerosol Spray)

12. How did the Ancient Egyptians move the huge stones they used
    to build the Pyramids? _____
    _____(Get your Bearings)

13. What did Charles Wilson design in 1872?_____(Solar Stills)

14. What fungal infection sometimes grows on our feet? _____ _____(Algae and Fungi)

15. Who discovered gravity in 1666? _____(Finding a Balance)

16. What was unusual about Leonardo da Vinci's notes? _____(Kaleidoscope)

17. How do spiders know they have trapped an insect in their webs? _____
    _____(Pitfalls and Pooters)

18. What percentage of the water in the world is seawater?_____(Solar Stills)

19. What causes acid rain and how does this rain affect crops? _____
    _____(Chemistry in the Kitchen)

20. What do workmen put on oil spills on the road to prevent skidding?_____(Slick Tricks)

SCORE ____ /20

SCIENTERRIFIC!

Are you scienterrific? Can you talk the talk? Show your understanding of the language of Science by filling in the blank spaces with the correct 'scientific' vocabulary. Check your answers by looking back at the chapters indicated.

1. Red cabbage water will tell you if a solution is an acid or a base because, like litmus paper, it is a good _____. (Chemistry in the Kitchen)

2. Foods that are rich in starch are often _____ food in poor countries. (Testing for Starch)

3. A crane uses a _____ to lift heavy objects. (The Electromagnet)

4. _____ is a highly skilled art form and can achieve very realistic results. (Aerosol Spray Gun)

5. Much of the wear and tear suffered by machinery is the result of _____ _____. (Get your Bearings)

6. Seeds need the proper conditions to _____. (Plant Detectives)

7. All objects, people and animals have a _____. This is their balancing point. (Finding a Balance)

8. German U-boats used a _____ to see above the surface of the sea. (The Kaleidoscope)

9. Unlike mammals, birds and fish, minibeasts are _____. (Pitfalls and Pooters)

10. Solar stills use the heat of the Sun to _____ water that is muddy or salty. (Solar Stills)

11. A tornado is a type of _____. (The Tornado Machine)

12. Many people use moisturising creams to _____ their skin. (Potato Power)

13. Oils are very good at reducing friction between materials as they _____ _____. (Slick Tricks)

14. Many gardeners spray their plants with _____ during hot, damp weather. (Algae and Fungi)

15. Millions of _____ of plants grow on Earth. (Plant Detectives)

SCORE ____ /15

Troubleshoot experiments

- A small but vital element is missing from each of these experiments.
- **Troubleshoot** the problem, and then draw and label what is 'missing'.
- **Explain** how each experiment should work, if properly set up.

Solar Stills

Explain

    (a) why the solar still is not working;

    (b) how it should work if properly set up.

_____

_____

_____

The Electromagnet

Explain

    (a) why the electromagnet is not working;

    (b) what a working electromagnet should do.

_____

_____

_____

The Kaleidoscope

Explain

    (a) what is missing from the kaleidoscope;

    (b) how a kaleidoscope should work.

_____

_____

_____

Pitfalls and Pooters

Explain

    (a) how a pooter works;

    (b) what is needed to complete this pooter.

_____

_____

_____